Spotlight on Climate Change

Climate Change and Extreme Weather

Isaac Kerry

Lerner Publications ✦ Minneapolis

To Lily and Julia

Lerner Publications Company
An imprint of Lerner Publishing Group, Inc.
241 First Avenue North
Minneapolis, MN 55401 USA

For reading levels and more information, look up this title at www.lernerbooks.com.

Main body text set in Adrianna Regular.
Typeface provided by Chank.

Editor: Cole Nelson

Library of Congress Cataloging-in-Publication Data

Names: Kerry, Isaac, author.
Title: Climate change and extreme weather / Isaac Kerry.
Description: Minneapolis : Lerner Publications, [2023] | Series: Searchlight books - spotlight on climate change | Includes bibliographical references and index. | Audience: Ages 8–11 | Audience: Grades 4–6 | Summary: "Why are some places flooding more than they used to? Why do hurricanes seem to get stronger every year? With engaging diagrams and photos, this book explores how climate change affects weather across the globe"— Provided by publisher.
Identifiers: LCCN 2021058575 (print) | LCCN 2021058576 (ebook) | ISBN 9781728457956 (library binding) | ISBN 9781728463926 (paperback) | ISBN 9781728461908 (ebook)
Subjects: LCSH: Climatic changes—Juvenile literature. | Climatic extremes—Juvenile literature.
Classification: LCC QC903.15 .K466 2023 (print) | LCC QC903.15 (ebook) | DDC 551.6—dc23/eng/20220120

LC record available at https://lccn.loc.gov/2021058575
LC ebook record available at https://lccn.loc.gov/2021058576

Manufactured in the United States of America
2-1009737-50162-5/31/2023

Table of Contents

Chapter 1

A CHANGING CLIMATE

Wildfires burning through the wilderness. Hurricane winds and waves surging over cities. Heat waves scorching the ground. It seems as if every year more and more extreme weather events are happening. This is because the world's climate is changing.

BIG WAVES HIT TEXAS DURING HURRICANE HARVEY IN 2017.

The word *climate* refers to the kind of weather a place usually has over a long period of time. Earth's climate has stayed about the same for the last eight thousand years. Warmer and cooler times have come and gone, but for the most part, Earth's climate has been stable. This has allowed human civilization to grow. That stability is coming to an end.

Scientists started keeping track of Earth's temperature in 1880. Every year since then the world has gotten warmer. The ten warmest years that humans have measured have happened in the past sixteen years. This warming of Earth's atmosphere is causing never-before-seen impacts to Earth's climate. Most of these changes will make life on Earth more difficult for humans.

GLOBAL AVERAGE SURFACE TEMPERATURE

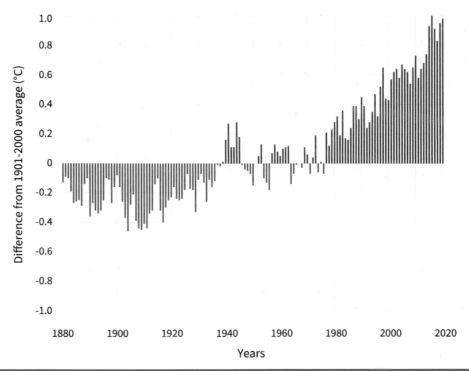

The blue bars show cooler-than-average temperatures, and the red bars show warmer-than-average temperatures.

STEM Spotlight

Most of the world measures temperature in degrees Celsius. This is also the way scientists talk about temperature. Any study talking about climate change will probably use Celsius. However, temperature in the United States is measured using Fahrenheit. Scientists who study climate change agree that people need to prevent Earth from warming more than 2.7°F (1.5°C). If it gets any warmer, then climate change could get much worse.

Chapter 2

HEAT, DROUGHT, AND FLAMES

Warming the world a few degrees does not seem as if it should make a huge difference. However, this increased temperature is the average for the world. Differences in climate and weather patterns mean some places will not change a huge amount. Other places will change much more. That means certain areas will deal with big problems from their new, hotter climates.

Heat Waves

A heat wave is a period of very high heat. They can last from a few days to several weeks. They can be extremely deadly. In 2003, a heat wave hit Europe. Over seventy thousand people died. More people die each year from heat in the US than any other weather event. By 2050, the number of high heat days in the US could triple. This puts more people at risk for a dangerous condition called heatstroke.

People try to stay cool during a heat wave in Paris.

Other areas of the world will get much hotter than the US. Some regions near the equator could see over 120 extra high heat days. This will make them practically impossible for humans to live in.

Heat waves have many other negative effects. People use more air-conditioning, which uses more energy. This leads to more greenhouse gases being created.

This riverbed in California has dried up because of heat waves and drought.

STEM Spotlight

Earth's climate has naturally changed over the last 4.5 billion years. But current climate change is different. Natural systems are not creating this change. Scientists agree that this is happening because of human activity. We burn fossil fuels to create electricity. This creates gases that go into the air. These greenhouse gases trap heat in the atmosphere and warm the planet. Only by reducing the amount of gases we create can we stop global warming and reduce climate change. One way to do this is by using renewable energies like solar or wind power.

Some important food crops cannot handle the extra heat. Livestock like cows will deal with many of the same health dangers humans do. This can create food shortages or even famines. High heat also dries out the land. This can create droughts.

DROUGHT HARMS A CALIFORNIA RANGE IN 2014.

Droughts

Droughts occur when there is much less rainfall than usual for a long time. This leads to drier ground and water shortages. Climate change causes droughts in two different ways. First, the hotter it is, the more water evaporates from the ground. Second, climate change

Droughts can damage crops, such as corn.

makes weather patterns shift. This means that some places in the world will get much less rain and snow than they have in the past.

Droughts are serious problems. They are the second most expensive climate event, behind only hurricanes.

Some countries are able to come up with the money to pay for the damages that climate events cause. But some countries have a much more challenging time. Over seven hundred million people around the world may be impacted by severe droughts by the year 2030.

Excessive heat and droughts can cause bodies of water to dry up all around the world.

The sky above San Francisco, California, is filled with smoke in 2020 as wildfires rage across the state.

Wildfires

Wildfires are a type of fire that happens in the wilderness. They happen every year in the summer, but climate change is making them worse. Warmer air removes moisture from the ground and from plants.

When heat waves and droughts occur, they add to this effect. This makes a big supply of small, very flammable fuel. This makes it easier for wildfires to start and allows them to grow much bigger.

This satellite image shows smoke from wildfires in California in 2017.

Wildfires destroy the natural landscape and can kill people caught in their path. They also can create serious health problems. The smoke they create causes air pollution. Research has shown this pollution causes hundreds of thousands of deaths each year.

Chapter 3

WIND AND WATER

Heat waves, droughts, and wildfires all make sense in a warmer world. But why will climate change also cause flooding and hurricanes? The answer lies in the ways the world's climate interacts with local weather systems. As Earth's atmosphere warms, winds shift and carry rain clouds to new places. As wind patterns shift, more extreme storms happen.

Coastal communities and island nations, such as Tuvalu, are at risk of flooding from rising sea levels as a result of climate change.

Flooding

While some areas will receive less rainfall due to climate change, other places will receive more. For example, in the northeastern United States storms make about 27 percent more rain than they did one hundred years ago. Looking ahead into the next hundred years, scientists predict there will be 50 percent more heavy rain.

Additionally, climate change is causing sea levels to rise. Since 1880, oceans all over the world have risen about 8 inches (20 cm). This makes it much easier for flooding to occur in coastal areas. Sea levels could rise as much as 2 to 7 feet (0.6 to 2.1 m) by 2100. This could make 410 million people all over the world have to find new homes.

In 2009, Maldives government members go underwater to sign a document urging countries to reduce their carbon dioxide emissions.

In 2018, the streets of Horry County in South Carolina are flooded after Hurricane Florence.

Hurricanes

Climate change will also cause stronger and more damaging hurricanes. Oceans absorb heat from the atmosphere. Warmer oceans make hurricanes with stronger wind speeds and help hurricanes create more rain. Both are serious problems for communities in their path. Stronger winds create much more damage, and more precipitation leads to flooding. Rising sea levels also help hurricanes become more dangerous. Storm surge is how much the ocean will rise during a storm. Since climate change is already leading to higher seas, this surge will be even more dangerous in future storms.

Scientists predict that for every 1.8°F (1°C) Earth's temperature rises, we will see 25 to 30 percent more serious hurricanes.

HURRICANE IDA BRINGS STRONG WINDS, RAIN, AND WAVES TO THE BORDER OF LOUISIANA AND MISSOURI IN 2021.

Chapter 4

LIVING WITH AN ANGRY PLANET

The evidence paints a clear picture: climate change is happening, and it is creating serious problems. Do we have to simply accept this new, angry planet? Or is there still time to avoid the worst changes? The answer is a little bit of both. If the world acts quickly, we can reduce the worst effects. However, some changes to Earth's climate are permanent. We will need to learn to adapt to these challenges.

The more greenhouse gases we put into the air, the worse climate change is going to be. Reducing these gases is the most important thing we can do to limit global warming. In 2016, the Paris Agreement was signed by most of the world's nations. This treaty sets a goal to keep warming to 2.7°F (1.5°C). This would mean the worst effects of climate change will not happen.

Greenhouse gases trap heat from the sun in Earth's atmosphere.

Disha Ravi

Disha Ravi is a climate activist from Bangalore, India. She is the founder of India's chapter of the Fridays for Future movement. This is an international movement led by young people. It tries to draw attention to climate change issues. Dashi has been especially focused on the concerns of India's farmers. In 2021, she was arrested because of her support for a farming protest. Her case was later dismissed in court. She continues to advocate for solving the climate crisis.

People protest the arrest of Disha Ravi in 2021.

In 2016, US secretary of state John Kerry signs the Paris Agreement.

By 2021, the world was not on track to keep that goal. If nothing changes, by 2100, the world will possibly be over 5.4°F (3°C) warmer. Extreme weather will become worse. But there is still time to make the needed changes. Many climate activists and scientists are working to reduce greenhouse gas emissions and create a healthier, happier planet for all.

You Can Help!

One way to reach out to other people about the climate is to write a letter to the editor for your local newspaper. There is no age limit or requirements to write one. If you get a few people to take action on climate change, that can make a big difference!

On a computer, search for the name of your local paper and the words "letter to the editor." This will usually take you to a web page where you can submit your letter. You can use this sample letter to get started:

Dear Editor:
My name is [NAME], and I am a [GRADE LEVEL] student in [TOWN]. I am writing because I am very concerned about the climate change crisis. This issue is important to me because [LIST TWO OR THREE EXAMPLES OF HOW CLIMATE CHANGE AFFECTS YOU OR YOUR TOWN].

I want people to know that they can help find a solution for our community and planet. Simple ways to help are to lower your carbon footprint by using less energy. You can also talk to your community leaders about making energy in ways that don't hurt the environment.

We can all do our part to fix climate change. I know that together we can make a difference.
Sincerely,
[NAME]

Glossary

average: a level that is typical, or a number calculated by adding quantities together and dividing the total by the number of quantities

emission: something that is given off or escapes into the atmosphere, such as gas

equator: the widest point on the globe

evaporate: when a liquid turns into a gas

famine: extremely short supplies of food

fossil fuel: a fuel that was created by plants and animals that died long ago

greenhouse gas: a gas that warms the planet when it is put into the atmosphere

heatstroke: a condition that happens when the body cannot manage its temperature in high heat

treaty: a legal agreement between two nations

Learn More

Herman, Gail. *What Is Climate Change?* New York: Penguin Workshop, 2018.

Kurtz, Kevin. *Climate Change and Rising Temperatures*. Minneapolis: Lerner Publications, 2019.

National Institute of Environmental Health Sciences: Climate Change
https://kids.niehs.nih.gov/topics/climate-change/index.htm

Weather Wiz Kids: What Is Climate?
https://www.weatherwizkids.com/weather-climate.htm

What's Climate Change? And What Can I Do?
https://www.climaterealityproject.org/blog/just-kids-what-climate-change-and-what-can-i-do

Woodward, John. *Climate Change*. New York: DK, 2021.

Index

Photo Acknowledgments

Image credits: American Prestige Deign/iStock/Getty Images, p. 5; NOAA, p. 6; AP Photo/
Franck Prevel, p. 9; USDA photo by David Kosling/flickr (CC BY 2.0), p. 10; USDA photo by
Cynthia Mendoza/flickr (CC BY 2.0), p. 12; CraneStation/flickr (CC BY 2.0), p. 13; piyaset/iStock/
Getty Images, pp. 14–15; Christopher Michel/flickr (CC BY 2.0), pp. 16–17; NASA, p. 18; Ashley
Cooper/Corbis/Getty Images, p. 20; AP Photo/Mohammed Seeneen, p. 21; U.S. Army National
Guard Photo by Staff Sgt. Roberto Di Giovin/flickr (CCO 1.0), pp. 22–23; Warren Faidley/Corbis/
Getty Images, p. 24; BlueRingMedia/Shutterstock.com, p. 26; REUTERS/Rupak De Chowdhuri/
Alamy Stock Photo, p. 27; AP Photo/Mary Altaffer, p. 28.

Cover: Dennis K. Johnson/Stockbyte/Getty Images.